FINISHING LINE PRESS

www.finishinglinepress.com

D0872987

ALPHAPOETICA

A Poetry Primer
for the Everyday Poet

poems by

Kate McCarroll Moore

Finishing Line Press
Georgetown, Kentucky

ALPHAPOETICA

A Poetry Primer
for the Everyday Poet

ACKNOWLEDGMENTS

With special thanks to poets
Amy Krause Rosenthal
Amy Ludwig VanDerwater
Georgia Heard
Kevin Hodgson
Naomi Shihab Nye
Ralph Fletcher
Richard Blanco
Tess Taylor

"Tossed from the Nest"; "A Little Bird Told Me"; "Winter Conversation"; and
"Benediction" previously published in *Avians of Mourning*, Finishing Line
Press, 2020

"Creation" previously published in *Digital Paper*, Issue 29

"the sweet swift passage of time" and "Nature Doesn't Seem to Know or
Care" previously published in *Through the Window: Voices of the Valley*, 2020
Anthology

Publisher: Leah Huete de Maines
Editor: Christen Kincaid
Cover Art: Photograph by Kate McCarroll Moore
Author Photo: Photographer, Nina Pomeroy
Cover Design: Elizabeth Maines McCleavy

Order online: www.finishinglinepress.com
also available on amazon.com

Author inquiries and mail orders:
Finishing Line Press
P. O. Box 1626
Georgetown, Kentucky 40324
U. S. A.

Table of Contents

For Bob, heart of my heart.

INTRODUCTION

The upside of sheltering at home during a pandemic is the time and space to shelter in poetry. Beginning and ending each day immersed in imagery brought comfort in the midst of chaos. The lyrical daily balm of Ambassador Daniel Mulhall reading snippets of Irish poetry in a lilting brogue on Twitter. The simple encouraging offerings for kids of all ages from Amy Ludwig VanDerwater at The Poem Farm. The topical, illustrated FaceBook poems posted by Lynn Ungar that speak to the moment. Their words brought calm and peace to my days.

Poetry allows me to breathe. To listen. To pay attention. To hope. To go on.

I've taken this time in solitude to reread my own poems and to consider my poetic influences and evolution. To reflect on poetry's impact on my life. Do I write poetry to make sense of the world? Or do I write poetry as a means of escape because the world in its current state does not make sense? Hard to tell.

What I do know is that throughout my life, poetry has been my go-to method of escape, expression, and exploration.

In my sixth-grade flowery handwriting I wrote a sappy poem about a butterfly landing on my nose. I was so very proud of myself and my craftmanship, especially that last line—"I wept." So dramatic! I loved that my teacher had me read it aloud, allowing me to gain firsthand knowledge of the importance of pace and pause. The realization that poetry is meant to be read aloud. Meant to be shared.

High school exposed my adolescent penchant for hyperbole. Love and drama entwined in hormonal angst.

Love's sweet nectar
Has been poured over us
In some strange mold
That causes us to cling together
Forever, as it should be

We have swallowed each other whole
Sing a eulogy to hunger!

Honestly, could it get any sappier?

Or this poem, published in the school's literary magazine that included the line, *It pierced a hole through the night, and she crawled through it*. So overwrought. It feels like it was drug-induced, but I assure you, it was not. I can still remember the sense of euphoria I felt writing it though.

She sat in solitude on the rocky coastline; head cradled in aching, stinging palms. She closed the door to her mind. She sat, knees pressed against her throbbing breasts; eyes fixed on the dark waves foaming and crashing at her side. She thought of nothing.

She glanced around to see the darkness closing in on her. Like four impenetrable walls, the night seemed to be drawing closer until it squeezed and gnashed at her small frame and she writhed in pain.

She let out a long, shrill, terrifying scream. It pierced a hole through the night, and she crawled through it.

She lay down on the crystal sand and jagged pebbles. A warmth overtook her delicate body. No thoughts disturbed her tranquil mind.

She awoke to the bright sunlight of a new day. Beautiful music filled the air and angels danced on by.

When I was pregnant with my first child (and listening to lots of Van Morrison thanks to my husband who kept *Astral Weeks* and *Veedon Fleece* on repeat), I wrote *Moondance*, a nine-line poem (one line per each month of pregnancy), which I proudly shared with my colleagues in the Capital District Writing Project. They thought it was a sex poem. My high school sensibilities still embarrassingly on display. It's fairly obvious that one of my early influences was Rod McKuen.

Moondance

Moonchild
every night you
put on a show for us
making my belly dance
soft silent waves
crest and fall
rhythmic pounding
fills the night
as we drift off

It wasn't until a college lit course that I fell in love with the romantic poets. Keats and Yeats. Blake and Coleridge. Wordsworth and Byron. I grew my poetic sensibilities, encouraged and enlightened by incredible professors like the late great William Dumbleton, and his dramatized recitation of Yeats' still relevant and powerful poem, *The Second Coming.*

Later still, I discovered the relatable work of contemporary poets like Naomi Shihab Nye and Billy Collins. *Kindness. The Names.* Poems that I've read hundreds of times, never failing to be knocked out by the powerful way they evoke empathy and heart.

The small poems of William Stafford and Emily Dickinson.
The spoken word of Sarah Kay and Shane Koyczan.
The social commentary of Bob Dylan and Jericho Brown.
The confessional whisperings of Ellen Bass and Robert Lowell.

So many influences, too many to recount.

My life has been shaped and enriched by the poets I've read. The poets I've heard. The poets I've met. The poets I've known. As you reflect on your poetry experiences, you'll likely come to understand and appreciate the way poets' words have informed your being. There's such transformative power in revisiting classic favorites and discovering emerging voices.

I've heard it said that like being struck by lightning or the proverbial lightbulb over the head, ideas that spark poetry suddenly appear from above. Poetry mused into being. I used to think that too.

But then, in a stroke of luck generated by my city's artistic vision, I was appointed to fill the time-honored position of Poet Laureate. Walking in the footsteps of poets such as Rita Dove, Juan Felipe Herrera, Robert Frost, Robert Hass, and Natasha Trethewey, I discovered a secret. Poems are born of invitation.

Being invited to write a poem, inspires the poem.

A Poet Laureate can't wait for inspiration to strike. *There's a groundbreaking Thursday, there's a grand opening Saturday, there's a citizen being honored tomorrow night*—the requests are random and diverse. The poem starts to take shape the moment a poet is approached with an invitation.

The invitation becomes that lightning bolt or lightbulb moment. The invitation is the inspiration.

This is a poetry primer—a collection of my small poems, presented for you thematically, in alphabetical order. Each entry begins with a brief description of my inspiration, followed by the poem that emerged, and finally, an invitation for you to give it a try. It's an invitation to enter the life of a working poet to share in the creative process of poetry making.

Please allow me to share my poetic inspirations, and an invitation to write your own life story in poetry.

Ready, set, begin.

Artifacts

Inspiration: I'm a collector, and I have always been fascinated by the ability of objects to hold story. As a child, the bottom drawer of my dresser was filled with found objects. A pencil stub, a small plastic baby doll, a gum wrapper necklace—things found on the ground, secreted into pockets, carried home to be sorted and stored. Objects of whimsy and wonder.

I lived in a constant state of imagining: Where did this come from? Who loved it? Who lost it? What has it witnessed?

As I grew up, my obsession continued to grow. Crossing the street with my brother in Manhattan, we were nearly flattened as I stopped dead in mid-town traffic to pick up a penny. On a weekend in Austin with my sister, I found a silver bracelet in the middle of an empty street, and slipped it onto my wrist. A puffy red heart in a snowbank in Albany, New York. An ancient rock loosed from a wall at the Colosseum in Rome. A broken brick from my daughter's backyard in Boston. An empty Dunhill's cigarette pack in Kilkenny, Ireland. A bottle cap from the hill overlooking Madonna's estate. A black 9-11 pin. A pink Barbie shoe. A discarded love note. A laminated picture of the Pope. A dented hubcap from the side of the road. A small rubber duck. A heart shaped stone.

Walking, I am constantly on the lookout. Last month, I carried home 3 unfinished bird's nests, an owl feather, 2 golf balls, a penny sheared in half, a small wrench, a rusty key. There they sit on my shelf, waiting for poems.

Messenger

I found a feather
stuck in the ground like a flag
    a gift from an owl

who called out my name
message dropped from the skygod
illegal to own

I carried it home
to remind me each new day
rules are for breaking

> though spirits are not

My daily walks turn into stories. Stories turn into poems. But not just my poems. They can be your poems too.

Invitation: I have canvas bags filled with the treasures I've found. I invite you to reach inside and choose an object. Allow the object to whisper its story to you. Write it down. See? You're a poet.

(Note: Experimenting with form is part of the process. The poem above is made up of three linked haiku.)

Birds

Inspiration: In April 2018, I met the writer Amy Ludwig VanDerwater through a twitter post inviting followers to celebrate National Poetry Month by exploring 1 subject 30 ways. Intrigued, I chose the topic of birds, and spent the next month crafting and posting bird poems, which Amy kept responding to and retweeting. Those poems became the inspiration for my first poetry chapbook, *Avians of Mourning*, when I realized I was really writing about my father. He was known as Birdmanmac, and we shared a love of nature—especially birds—a fact that came through loud and clear in my poems.

Tossed from the Nest

The first time
I rescued a bird
I was eight years old
Playing tag in Joey Hughes' yard

I stopped when he yelled freeze
Looked down at my feet
And there, beside my scuffed Keds
A nearly naked bird

Everything froze in that moment
While I gathered
Shoebox
Tissue pillow
Eyedropper
Me

In my mind, the bird
took rest and sustenance
Grew feathers
Learned to fly
Brought its chicks to meet me
The girl who saved a life

Instead, despite my nursing
And desperate prayers

A different fate, life lesson learned
My father's steady hand, my shaking shoulders
His words resounding
Nothing you could have done
Happens every day
Other mouths to feed
Only the strong survive

A Little Bird Told Me

When I was 16
my boyfriend bought me a parrot
and a cage to keep him in

I wanted a lovebird
Played a record day and night
teaching that caged bird to talk
Hello, baby, want a kiss?
Hello, baby, want a kiss?
The bird just squawked!

Pulled his feathers out
one by one
refused to speak
barked like a dog
Still, I didn't understand
the misery of not being allowed to fly.

Invitation: I chose birds as my topic. But you can choose anything your heart desires. Block out the next thirty days on your calendar and commit to revisiting that topic 30 ways. Pay attention to other themes or stories that may emerge in your poetry collection.

Collective Memoir

Inspiration: I had the good fortune of meeting the late Amy Krause Rosenthal a few times; once when my daughters and I astoundingly were the only people to show up at a book signing in Berkeley, and a few years later when I wrote to her about my success using her picture book, *This Plus That*, in a research project with first grade teachers. Her response included this wonderful line: *Your letter + Receiving + Pondering = JOY.*

In 2016 she was scheduled to be the special guest at a "summer camp for grownups" hosted by Rakestraw Books, the local independent bookstore in Danville, California. A few weeks before that event was to take place, Amy called Mike Barnard, the bookstore owner, to say her health had taken a turn, and she could no longer travel. You can imagine how hard it was for her to bow out of something like that. My friend Mike wanted to honor what she had planned to present, and so he asked me if I would run Amy's session. I was privileged to do so, and Amy was grateful that the event would go on without her.

One of the activities we did that day was to write a collective memoir 'a la Amy. The idea is presented in her marvelous *Textbook* (Dutton, 2016).

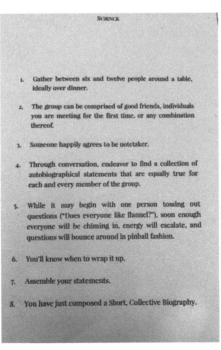

SCIENCE

1. Gather between six and twelve people around a table, ideally over dinner.

2. The group can be comprised of good friends, individuals you are meeting for the first time, or any combination thereof.

3. Someone happily agrees to be notetaker.

4. Through conversation, endeavor to find a collection of autobiographical statements that are equally true for each and every member of the group.

5. While it may begin with one person tossing out questions ("Does everyone like flannel?"), soon enough everyone will be chiming in, energy will escalate, and questions will bounce around in pinball fashion.

6. You'll know when to wrap it up.

7. Assemble your statements.

8. You have just composed a Short, Collective Biography.

Here's the poem we wrote together that first day of summer camp. I've since taught this memoir session to many groups, from middle schoolers to graduate students to work colleagues and it's always a successful and enlightening experience. Best of all, I always feel Amy there in the room with us. Her spirit lives on.

A Collective Memoir, inspired by Miss Amy K.R.

We are nine well-traveled women sitting in a circle in a stranger's backyard
at the top of a late-summer hill
reflecting on the world we left behind for a day
feeling an overwhelming sense of gratitude
and appreciation for this moment
in this wonderful, and sometimes too chaotic life

All have walked on distant beaches,
felt the sand between our toes
stood at the base of a giant redwood
cooked with color, exercised our bodies and our minds
and read books that have changed us

We've felt the power of first love,
said I love you in the moment
held someone's hand through sorrow
shared uncontrollable laughter
and gone road tripping

We've all found ourselves lost at times
but today we are found,
feeling a powerful connection to nature, the great outdoors
and something greater than ourselves
our lives now intertwined, new friendships cultivated by a local bookseller
and a belief in that simple truth, revealed by Anne Frank,
that people are really good at heart
despite everything

Invitation: Gather some family or friends or a group of strangers, follow Amy's recipe, and write a poem together. In the wonderful creative spirit of the wonderfully creative Amy, feel free to improvise.

Conversation

Inspiration: I remember exactly where I was. Sitting at my desk, in the den, on a work night, chatting with my dad. Unusual, because most of the time phone calls home were between me and my mom—she, animatedly reporting all the gossip and family news, while dad quietly breathed on the other line. But this night, she was out with her sisters when I called, and he felt like chatting. We had a longish conversation about family and local events and the differences between weather in California (bright, warm, skyblue, perfect), and weather back home (grey, cold, rainy, typical), and then he said it, so mater-of-factly: *Time is running out.* I wish I would have taken a cue from that and engaged in a real heart-to-heart, but I didn't. I just left it hanging there. And then after I hung up, this emerged.

Winter Conversation

Time is running out
my father said last night
his words dropped with regret
into our casual conversation about the weather
It's the hard, inevitable truth
that lives in every moment,
propels us forward
with such urgency
and denial, as if we could outrun the clock

On my walk today I imagine
this neighborhood a thousand years from now
tourists scavenging for a shard of glass, a remnant
of this time

They'll piece together what they can of us

All of this means so much
and nothing at all

Or this poem, the response to an anxious text message from a child.

Summer Storm

The sky this morning. Streaked with yellow.
Clouds of grey smoke hang still above
hilltops where lightning lit the night
and thunder rolled and roared. Common
enough in the Midwest, but here this
California August, shimmering
air distorts my view. My daughter texts
an urgent message. *Is the world ending?* How
can I answer in truth when Death
Valley records the hottest day on earth,
and even songbirds refuse to sing?

Invitation: When someone tells you something poignant, personal, or profound, find a quiet place to reflect and gather your thoughts. If you're asked a question that has no answer, jot it down, let it simmer. Let whatever emotion you're feeling drive the writing of the poem. And then, most importantly, continue the conversation.

Crossword

Inspiration: In 2014, I was invited to teach a poetry workshop in Spokane, Washington at the Northwest Inland Writing Project Annual Spring Conference. The session I shared was *Exploring the Poetry of Place and the Place of Poetry*, which draws on memory and always yields remarkably rich and candid poetry. At the session's close, one of the participants in my workshop was high school English teacher, Paul Bonnell. On his way out, he handed me this index card, which I treasure. He had made a crossword poem of thanks. This, he told me, is how he captures the main points he wants to remember. His creativity and kindness is something I will never forget.

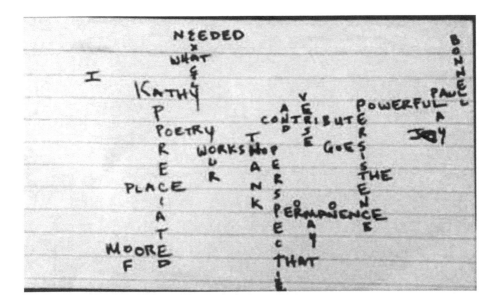

Invitation: As you read or watch or listen to something that interests you, jot down words or phrases that resonate. Afterwards, create a crossword poem using the words you've selected.

Dance

Inspiration: During my tenure as Poet Laureate, I was invited to write and read poetry on many occasions across many settings. When a local dance company was putting together their next performance, the director thought it would be cool to choreograph a dance to a poem. I thought so too.

Dance is poetry. There's the language of movement. There's rhythm. Structure. Punctuation. White space. Passion.

The music chosen was a song by Sia. I used her words and emotion as source material. On stage it was a magical collaboration. The poet, reading. The dancer, dancing. The music, soaring.

For You

All poetry is prayer, the poet says,
Lifting eyes to the sky
The rhythm clinging to each heartbeat
In the white space
That breathes beyond and between
Each syllable, each sentiment, each word,
Spoken and unspoken

All dance is poetry, the dancer mimes
Mouthing the words to the song inside
One heartbeat matching each beat of the drum
Each run of the keys, timed, syncopated,
A marriage of movement and might
The language of love and longing

Dance is poetry, poetry is prayer
In the space beyond and between
A story told in silence, melody and grace
The dancer's spirit bent and broken, healed and saved.

The dancer's stage, an altar
Where truth hides in the shadows
Is anybody out there listening?

The dancer's arms, a symbol
Outstretched, pleading, prayerful, strong
Are you coming to get me now?

Dance of sorrow, dance of praise
Can you hear my call?
Here I am, on my knees
Can you see me now?
When will you find the space to
Answer me, rescue me, deliver me.

Watch me dance out loud

Invitation: Put on some music. Bounce a line or two off the lyric and the melody. Turn your sparked lines into a poem. Close your eyes and picture the movement. Get up and dance. Feel the rhythm. Move to the beat of your heart.

Echo

Inspiration: The first time I went to a CATE (California Association of Teachers of English) Conference, I lucked into a session taught by teacher Daniel Alderson, sharing the strategy described in his book *Talking Back to Poems: A Working Guide for the Aspiring Poet* (Celestial Arts, 1996). I have used and taught this strategy hundreds of times since that fateful day. This was my initial attempt.

Original Poem	**Echo Poem**
The Cold Room—Yvor Winters	**The Long Night—Kate Moore**
The dream	The moon
stands	rises
in the night	in the silence
above unpainted	above unpainted
floor and chair.	lake and hill.
The dog is	The day is
dead asleep	dead asleep
and	and
will not move	will not move
for god or fire.	for God or man.
and from the	And from the
ceiling	heavens
darkness bends	starlight swallows
a heavy flame.	a heavy earth.

Invitation: Imitation is the sincerest form of flattery. Find a poem that you love. Read it slowly, carefully, noticing everything. Copy the poem in its entirety, staying true to white space, rhythm, punctuation, structure. Write a poem of your own that echoes the copied poem.

(Note: the poems of William Carlos Williams work especially well for this exercise. I have a whole collection of poems echoing *This is Just To Say* and *The Red Wheelbarrow* that have been posted on social media.)

Ekphrastic

Inspiration: I took a class on this poetic form from Tess Taylor in order to explore the genre more deeply. Ekphrastic poems can best be described as odes to art. In Tess's class we took a field trip to San Francisco Museum of Modern Art where we were encouraged to spend the evening wandering until we found a painting, photograph or sculpture that called to us. Tess told us this would be an exercise of pure love. I stood mesmerized before an Orozco painting. My heart leapt. This was it.

Sleeping (the family)   José Clemente Orozco, 1930

Silent Night, Holy Night

"Painting…it persuades the heart." (Orozco)

My eye is drawn first to the blue,
most radiant hue
robing this woman, a mother,
in warmth, the color of Mary
she is turned toward the father, his face bathed in heavenly light
asleep on the earthen floor of this makeshift shelter

Soft folds of blanket envelope them
where they lie together
two exhausted parents
too exhausted to hear the song of their daughter
wide awake now

lullabying a song she learned from them
as they moved from field to field
carrying pots of clay, red as the earth

How did she come to be,
this beautiful child, the color of the earth they work,
the earth they love?
What joy, what migrant passion called her forth
to walk beside them in the light and sing a night song
unafraid

This is another, written in response to one of my favorite paintings.

A Beautiful World   **Grandma Moses, 1948**

Creation

In a Vermont gallery
twenty years ago
I splurged on
a beautiful world
to hang above my bed

each morning I'm awakened
by visions of Grandma Moses
an old woman
working oils into dark wood
awakened

now, not yet as old
I've begun
to see with artist's eyes
painting in silence
waiting for poems
It's a prayerful meditation
to place a small pallet on the table
and begin

finding hidden shapes
and shades within a leaf
all of nature, a metaphor

I dip my brush into the water
colors becoming other colors
bright specks spreading quickly, bleeding hope

Life bursting into light

Invitation: Head to a gallery or museum (or an art book or internet website). Pay attention to your heartbeat—when it quickens, stop. Stare until you are sure it's love. Sit down and write a poem setting the scene and expressing the emotion that honors the work before you.

Fire

Inspiration: California is on fire. Days upon days upon days of nothing but sunshine and blue skies give way to scorching heat and wind and orange air. We wake to eerie daylight darkness and falling ash. In the midst of the devastation, poems arise with urgency to take shape on the page.

Another Autumn

mature majestic oaks
that line the unpaved path,
bend toward each other
in the almost light

nearly touching, just not quite

I walk alone this autumn morn
strewn with broken branches, brittle
chunks of jagged shredded bark
curled browned leaves
loosed by last night's wind
crunching underfoot

while warm winds made of smoke
deny the sky's true nature—
vines lie broken bent buried
in a fine thin dust of ash
carried here from distant fires

burning
      destroying
            transforming
                  renewing

I walk with purpose
my skin is tree bark—
not the polished sheen of beech
but the crusted stuff of old growth
blemished now and deeply grooved

fire-scarred, still standing
strong

I've seen my share of autumns
I've lived through fire too

On the nineteenth anniversary of the terrorist attacks of 9/11, I walked outside
to find the garden grey with ash from fires burning a hundred miles away.

Falling

such fine ash
coating the tomatoes
scattered from a burning sky

think about it
the poet said
this ash was once a tree
a bear, a bird, a man

the poet said
just think about it
on this day in history
smoke and ash filled another sky

ash that was once a dream
airplanes, buildings, babies
drifting down among the living—
souls mingling in remembrance

we are made of dust

to dust we shall return

Invitation: The world is on fire in so many ways. Focus your intention on
something that seems to be raging out of control. Pause to reflect and offer a
simple prayer. Turn your inward thoughts into a poem.

Found

Inspiration: I was walking through the neighborhood on trash day. There was a crumpled note on someone's lawn, beneath the bushes. I bent to pick it up and drop it in my neighbor's bin, but curiosity got the best of me. I unfolded a tattered page, torn from a notebook, and a shiver passed through me.

Ritual/Spellwork

crumpled sheet
found in the street
day after last
new moon

handwritten spell
outside the lines

I continuously transcend
into my evergrowing divine self
in my journey toward health and wholeness.

Long night's
lunar incantation

Burn
Burn
Burn

candles must be red
it said, for the spells to work

red flame licking
the page

names must be released
into the night sky

Invitation: When you come across an interesting note, or letter, or page, pull some words and phrases and arrange them to make a new poem. Other ways to make a found poem—take a marker and cross out all the words you don't want until you're left with something completely new, and all your own. Or take scissors to a text, cut out the words you like, and arrange them in different ways until a poem emerges. Find a new story inside someone else's words.

Ghosts

Inspiration: I traveled to a conference with my friend. We were sharing a room, sleeping side by side in twin beds. I woke up to the sound of her footsteps padding to the bathroom before I felt hot breath on my face and a repeated whisper in my ear. *"Are you willing to walk with me?"* I sat bolt upright, only to find my friend sound asleep in her bed. I lay there frozen, watching the air swirl and dance in waves across the room. In the morning, I tentatively approached the woman at the check-in counter and asked her if anyone had ever reported seeing a ghost. Her eyes widened as she asked what room I was in. Apparently, years before, a young girl had risen from her bed here, and walked straight into the ocean, never to be seen again. If I didn't believe in ghosts before, I do now.

Waiting for an Answer

Old smoke lingers
in the trees
swirling skyward
in the first breath of morning

glass-like calm
close and warm
whispers to me

I want, I want

Old voices linger
in the darkness
murmuring low
beneath the stillness
of dead asleep

Are you willing to walk with me?
Are you willing to walk with me?

Invitation: Think about something you've seen or heard that can't be explained through reason or logic. See if you can capture the mystery in the shape of a poem.

Grief

Inspiration: I was lying in bed, reading *H is for Hawk* by Helen Macdonald (Grove Press, 2014). This amazing book deals with the author's grief over the untimely death of her father, and I had just read the line, *"But now my father had died. Hold tight,"* when the phone rang. It was my brother, telling me that our father was dead. I sat up the rest of the night, hugging the book, unable to sleep. Unable to breathe. I was three thousand miles from home. Overcome with grief, I wrote a poem. I found Macdonald on twitter the next day, and sent her my poem along with this message, *"I was reading this line when the phone rang Tuesday night. First and last sentences are yours. Thank you."* Within an hour, she replied with heartfelt condolences. It made me feel our souls and our paths and our grief somehow connected, and that helped.

GRIEF

But now my father had died.
Hold tight.
Hold tight.
The words on the page stung.
Something far away
something too familiar.

Suddenly
this memoir in my hands—
love and bereavement tangled,
laid open, raw and bare.

A late-night phone call.
My father had died.
Right then.
A moment earlier, he was himself
old and tired, but alive
in the world
and then he was not.

Hold tight.
I closed the book.
Stared into the yellow eyes of the hawk before me.

This one was written a few years later, still dealing with that same emotion.

Ghost
I found a photograph in a drawer
the three of us captured, bound by time
in living color
my father leaning forward
strapped into a wheelchair
his eyes already dead
the rest, soon to follow

Captured in that in-between stage
where he'd been wheeled along a linoleum hallway
by aides who speak in accents
dripping of far away places
whispering this is just like home—
this narrow bed, this cramped, shared space
that's always dark

Home, he had a garden and an easy chair
where he'd read in afternoon sun
whistle as he filled bird feeders
sing a young man's songs as spring plants
took root
days and days and days
before

The photograph is a lie.
There are three of us pictured here.
But one of us is already a ghost.

Invitation: We all have loss and grief in our lives. Spend some time recalling one of those times. Try to craft a poem that expresses the pain. Trust that it will make it hurt a little less.

Heritage

Inspiration: I was not born in Ireland. My parents weren't either. Nor my grandparents. Nor theirs. We trace our Irish immigration story back generations. And yet... The first time I visited Ireland, I was dumbstruck. Looking out the windows of the airplane over Dublin, I felt a sensation I'd never felt landing anywhere before. Home. That's all I could think—I'm home. Every man on the street looked like my grandfather. Every store clerk was my cousin. The streets, alleys, shops, all felt so eerily familiar. I know this place, I thought. I've been here before.

Funny story. At the time of my first visit there, I was writing a weekly column for the local newspaper. While in Ireland, I wrote about the people we met along the way. In Kilkenny, I took a photo of two round-faced, red-headed, freckled boys sticking their heads out of a window in a little shed by the water. I submitted it along with a photo of a girl taking fiddle lessons and a man driving a pedicab. The next week, my article ran along with the photo of the two boys. The caption read *Moore's two sons, Steven and Andrew.* To this day, I wonder who they are, and if they ever knew their lives were forever linked to mine through an errant caption.

Ireland pulls at my heart. Below is *Trilogy*, a series of three linked poems from my last visit.

Trilogy

Changeling

The sea churns green below
and there are sheep along the runway
I imagine changelings here, as we skid to a stop
no words
just
the odd sensation of home
in this place
I've never been

Home.

in the place they left
driven out by famine
propelled by hope
their blood
runs through me
and recognizes home

Home.

In the morning
I'll get up early
walk to the corner cafe
buy an Irish Times
order tea
and pretend to read the news
imagining this kind of life
imagining home

Home.

You have the map of Ireland on your face
they said when I was growing up.
I'll take you home again, Kathleen
my father sang
he sang *tura lura lural*
that's an Irish lullaby

I'll Take You Home Again, Kathleen

Walking the streets of Dublin, I see my grandfather everywhere
The shock of white hair and the prominent chin
The eyes that twinkle like a cliché
There he sits in Kennedy's and at the bus stop next to Oscar Wilde
He's the doorman in silk top hat and tails
opening the taxi door outside the Merrion Arms
He's playing fiddle on the steps of St. Ann's

I am here in this place his father left
Driven out by famine, the terrible hunger

Propelled by hope, the great hunger

He came across the ocean, my grandfather's father
Packed in steerage for a month with the dead and the dying
So that my grandfather could be born
And sit in his house drinking tea, spooning marmalade
Giving life to my father who gave life to me

So that I could make a one day voyage in business class
Watching movies, sharing a three course meal
Knowing nothing of sacrifice and suffering
Still hungry, longing for home

Alone in the Dublin Writers Museum

Outside, a steady rain
pounds on leaded windows
in haunted Parnell Square
awakening
the ghosts of Behan, Beckett
Swift and Wilde

I wander hallways in fading light
A specter moving slowly
across splintered floors
opening doors that creak
and moan,
revealing rare and ancient manuscripts,
gathering dust in dusty rooms
a trove of leathered, weathered
artifacts, left open and untouched

Silenced voices, now released,
whirl from floor to ceiling
Dracula and Sweet Molly Malone
Alive, alive, oh, once again
swirling
rattling
crying out

the center cannot hold
just me
and all these ghosts

Invitation: Where are you from? Where have you felt most at home in the world? Picture yourself there once more. What are you doing? Thinking? Feeling? Capture that scene in a poem.

Home

Inspiration: On a visit back to my old hometown, we drove by my grandparent's house and a flood of memories came back in a whoosh.

I can picture every corner of every room. The yellow jar on the hall table filled with chiclets gum, the book shelf lined with little glass animals, the gold anniversary clock atop the television cabinet, the telephone table with its black rotary phone, the empty wine decanter, the china cabinet won in a card game, the skeleton key resting in the beveled glass door.

McArdle Avenue

My grandparents built their first home a century ago
before the wars and the death of their oldest son
in an area known as Arbor Hill,
the name suggesting leafy greenness,
expansive gardens,
rolling hills harboring
politicians
lumber barons and patricians

They had a small green patch of lawn out front
and a backyard garden of peonies and roses
edged with mint and chives
and rows of succulents they called hens and chicks

Inside, light streamed through stained glass in the hallway
separating two sets of gleaming wooden stairs—one leading up to the bedroom
where my father slept as a boy
the other leading to the dark basement
housing an old wringer washer
where I caught my arm while playing

On the porch I held a seashell to my ear
And heard the roaring ocean call
while my grandmother polished two flights of stairs
on hands and knees, her penance for those things she could not stop

One hundred years is a long time
One hundred years is the blink of an eye

Compelled, we drove by the house last winter,
before the pandemic, before the funeral of their youngest son
in an area known as Arbor Hill
the name suggesting
gunfire, drug deals, and urban blight
where fractured light casts dusty shadows on the past
where ghosts wander silently from room to room

And this reflects the house where my mother grew up.

Portrait of An Artist as a Young Girl

There's a patch of sunshine
on the sidewalk
in front of number 24
if you look closely
you can see the shadow
of an artist there
becoming

She's blooming there
where soft green pokes up
between the cobblestones
storing memories
of walks to school
and summer nights
spent on the stoop

She's growing there
where the painted clapboard
fades and peels
and the winter wind
rattles the glass
in her small, shared room

where she's never alone

She's dreaming there
where the treetops bend
under the weight of city birds
while she imagines her life's work
ahead of her, creating
a family made with love
brushed with her smile
painted with her laugh
drawn from her heart

She's painting there
at the kitchen table
in an artist's studio
in her waking hours
and her wildest dreams
brush and palette
color, life, and love
spilling wild across the canvas

Invitation: Find a photograph or make a quick sketch of a home that was special to you as a child. Close your eyes and open the front door. Walk yourself from room to room in your mind's eye. What remains the same? What has likely changed? Turn your wanderings and your wonderings into a poem where the past and the present collide.

Instruction

Inspiration: I have been a teacher my entire adult life. To introduce a professional learning session for educators on the magic of teacher—student relationships, my colleague, Robert Alpert, suggested that I focus on the importance of respect. This poem came out in one stream of consciousness draft, thinking about my own classroom. It has been used in dozens of education settings hence, even though some of the references inside are dated.

Respect

Step back for a moment, teacher
Give up your spot there
At the front of the room
At the head of the class
Turn off the overhead
Close your book
Put down that red pen and look around

Make your way to the empty desk
In the back of the room
Sit down
Quietly

Become now the boy who can't sit still
Who keeps his socks
And his belt
And his torn worksheets
Crumpled in a heap in the deep of his desk
His desk that creaks each time he lifts the lid
Tipping over unexpectedly at least once each
And every day
See the world now through his eyes

Take a seat there where the blue-haired girl sits
With her pierced nose and her glazed eyes
And her thoughts of death and suicide
And remember a house where there is no rest
And there is no peace

And there is no joy
Calling to you at the end of each
And every day
Hear the world now through her ears

Take a seat in your brown skin, in your gay skin
In your yellow skin, in your wrong skin

Fade out

Stand up, teacher
Move back
To the front
Can you see what's there before you?
Can you hear what is unspoken?
The heart of the matter
Beats out a rhythm of want
Loud
Against the classroom walls

Rise up, teacher
Rise up
Breathe the world slowly
More deeply now
Reach beyond what you think
You know
Remember why
You chose this

Discover who
They might be
Uncover what
They will be
When you rise up
And light up
The way

Invitation: You don't have to be a teacher to write a poem of advice and encouragement. What do you feel passionately about that you want to convey the importance of to others? Write that.

Jazz

Inspiration: When a swing band was hired for a concert at the local Performing Arts Center, the city's arts council approached me to see if I'd like to collaborate on a mash-up of sorts. The band and I would share the stage and alternate jazz songs with jazz poems, back and forth in concert. The band gave me their set list and I wrote a series of poems to complement the lyrics. This is one that was particularly fun to perform. I'd read a stanza—the horns would wail, back and forth in a jazzy rhythm.

Call and Response

I want to hear it hear it hear it
That mournful wailing cry
Telling my roots to wake up
Stirring my soul with jazz
Yeah, bring me back to jazz

I want to feel it feel it feel it
Blood coursing through my veins
My heart belongs to jazz

Slide that old trombone, man
Answer with your soul
Hear it, feel the rhythm
My feet, they love that jazz band
Yeah, my feet are cool with jazz

River flows within us
Running wild and free
Blow that trumpet, jazzman
Answer from down deep

Connect us all to jazz, man
Syncopate the beat
Syncopate the beat
Syncopate the beat
This jazz, it's made of heat.

Invitation: Try something new, maybe out of your comfort zone. Collaborate with a musician friend. Perform a call and response in your living room or on the stage. Wear a beret!

Key

Inspiration: Before she entered the nursing home, my grandmother pressed the skeleton key into my hand. It unlocked the china cabinet my grandfather won in a card game, along with the holiday china and all my childhood memories of Sunday dinner spent listening to stories of my father as a boy. How he pulled the chair out from under Mrs. Pompeli Reed just as she sat. How he pitched a perfect game. How he swam in Lake Luzerne the day before his brother drown. How he got reprimanded by a Christian Brother with a book smacked hard against his head. The key to my childhood opened the key to his childhood. And when I added it to my artifact teaching bag it opened the key to Jazmin's childhood too.

Continuation High School Blues

Classroom.
Six angry students. Hoods up. Earbuds in. Frowns set.
We're going to write today, I say.
We all have stories, I say.
It will be fun, I say.
Six angry students. Hoods up. Earbuds in. Frowns set.
Reach inside the bag, I say.
Take any object, I say.
Let it speak to you, I say.

Six angry students. Hoods up. Earbuds in. Frowns set.
Jazmin reaches in, reluctantly.
Drops my key unto her desk.
Puts her head down.
The clock ticks.
The bell rings.
Jazmin remains.

The room is empty.
Except for me.
And Jazmin.

She lifts her head.
Opens her notebook.

Grabs her pen.

Words fly across the page.
Lines ink from top to bottom.
Another page. And another.
Shoulders shake. Tears fall.
Pen rests on the desk, next to the key.

The room is empty.
Except for me.
And Jazmin.

She tilts her head.
Holds out her notebook.
Here, she says.

She was in fourth grade.
Her family lived together then.
Mother, father, brothers, Jazmin.
Snuggled together on the couch.
Sharing a moment.
Sharing a movie.
The Indian in the Cupboard.
A magic key. Time travel.
Fantasy. Family.
Once Upon a Time.

The clock ticks.
The bell rings.
Jazmin remains.

Invitation: Keys open doors. What keys have you held? What did they open? Where did they lead? What did you discover inside? Write a poem describing what was hiding behind a locked door.

List

Inspiration: I've been inspired to write list poems by prompts and colleagues in many different poetry sessions, but my favorite inspiration came from my poet friend, Georgia Heard. So simple, she just said, "Write a list poem. It can be about anything." I had the news on in the background. I started with a list of verbs contrasting this leader with another—the poem just sort of wrote itself.

When the news was just the news

For eight years
You modeled leadership
Standing tall in your tan suit
Sitting sure against a floral metaphor*
Walking proud into St. John's
Your girls by your side
Breaking soulfully into Amazing Grace, your voice soaring and straining
Pausing to catch your breath and dab your eyes
In yet another eulogy
The poetry of your voice
That rhythmic cadence
Each word chosen carefully
To lift and praise and unify

(*Note: the flowers in Obama's portrait symbolize his life: African blue lilies, Hawaiian jasmine, Chicago chrysanthemums.)

Invitation: I'll keep it simple, like Georgia did. Write a list poem. It can be about anything.

Mentors

Inspiration: When Richard Blanco was named as the 2013 inaugural poet, the Pulitzer Prize-winning poet Tracy K. Smith said that the White House had made an ideal choice, citing the scope of his poems and "their beautiful fidelity to private experience, to place, to community and to a complex sense of self." Here's my favorite section of the poem, the powerful last lines that Blanco delivered on that biting cold day in Washington.

And always one moon
like a silent drum tapping on every rooftop
and every window, of one country—all of us—
facing the stars
hope—a new constellation
waiting for us to map it,
waiting for us to name it—together.

Blanco's words inspired my poem, delivered on a not so cold January day in California celebrating the installation of the city's mayor:

One San Ramon, Our San Ramon

Every day, I step outside under the blue-black sky of early morning
Bare feet, cold concrete
The local paper waiting silently
Flung there by some mysterious unseen hand
I pause to look above,
Count the stars, name the ones I know,
Polaris, Ursa, Orion
And whisper a grateful thanks to the ever-present moon
Changing shape each night as it dances across this winter sky

How lucky we are to live in this valley
In the shadow of Mount Diablo
Where pioneers and farmers and family men
Stopped to plant and build and grow
Laying the foundation for this time and this place we love
This place we know as home

Home to tenth-generation Californians, and next generation citizens
All united in our love of this place,
Quality schools, welcoming churches and a cathedral of fresh air
Here we give thanks for plentiful parks and fields and miles of trails,
Rushing streams that appear after big rains,
And hillsides flecked with wildflowers and families
We worship light poles dotted with sentry-like hawks
Shady-treed medians and wide-open spaces
Festivals and fireworks and farmer's markets
Places to greet and gather and return to often
Reminding us all of our shared sense of pride
Our community and commitment
Our San Ramon, One San Ramon
Home

Invitation: Listen to the words of someone you admire. Study the way they speak. Let them be a mentor. Write a poem inspired by their voice.

Neighborhood

Inspiration: At Asilomar, I took a weekend class from Naomi Shihab Nye. In the first session, she asked us to draw a map of our neighborhood and label the important parts. I drew my house in Buffalo and the living room where I watched Sonny and Cher perform on the Lloyd Thaxton show. I drew the lilies of the valley growing beside the rock border in the front yard, the driveway where we played circle hopscotch, the backyard with the roller stored in the tool shed. Next door was the Schratz's house with their backyard tree fort and the row of bushes where the boys trapped bees in baby food jars. As I mapped out the neighborhood, stories swirled in my head. A few years later in Portland, Oregon, Ralph Fletcher expanded on the map idea by asking us to label the place where danger lurked.

Snakes and Strangers

At the end of the block
sat a small weedy field
wedged between houses
and the Mobil station
where I rode my bike alone
to spend my allowance on Baby Ruth's
and watch men in blue coveralls
covered with grease
slide underneath cars

After dinner we hid
among pussy willows
wielding long sticks
hunting for snakes
that we hoped not to find

At the far edge of the field
behind a stand of tall trees
a rusty trailer lurked
while we mapped out a plan

we'd tiptoe up slowly
knock, run, and hide

hearts pounding wildly
sticks at the ready
till our mothers called us home

Invitation: Revisit your childhood neighborhood in your mind's eye. Map your memories, allowing each story to emerge. (Add a place of danger if you're feeling brave). X marks the spot. Turn your map into a poem.

Oulipost

Inspiration: OULIPOST was a 2014
National Poetry Month project promoted by
the sadly now defunct Found Poetry Review.
Throughout that April, approximately 70
poets from around the globe were
selected to participate, applying strategies
sourced from the *Ouvroir de littérature potentielle* founded by mathematician
François Le Lionnais and the writer Raymond Queneau. The project's goal
was to illustrate how constraint fosters creativity. I was one of the lucky poets
selected to respond to each daily prompt and post the results on my blog. My
source text was *The Contra Costa Times*, my local newspaper.

"Oulipost #17: Haikuisation. Haikuisation has sometimes been used by
Oulipians to indicate the reduction of verses of normal length to lines of haiku-
like brevity. Select three sentences from a single newspaper article and "haiku"
them."

Spring
All the fields blossomed
Unfolding beautifully
Re-dedicated

Sourced from *The Contra Costa Times*, Bay Area News Group, April 17, 2014.
(SRV grads bolster Chabot baseball, Matt Schwab.)

"Oulipost #18: HOMOCONSONANTISM. Choose a sentence or short passage
from your newspaper to complete a homoconsonantism. In this form, the
sequence of consonantsin a source text is kept, while all its vowels are replaced."

THSLNCSNTRBSRSDFNNGTHYRR

Amen

This holy silence lingers,
cresting nightly,
rebounding, soaring, ascending
further

into hungry mouths of prayer,
repenting

Sourced from The Contra Costa Times, Bay Area News Group,
April 18, 2014. ('Tribes' delivers loud and clear, Karen D'Souza)

Invitation: Use these two prompt examples, or, even better, come up with your own rules for restraint. It is amazing what happens in your poet's brain when you are forced to follow arbitrary rules of engagement.

Postcard

Inspiration: The day we visited Walt Whitman's home on Long Island, it was closed. We peered dejectedly in the windows as the rain poured down. And then, as if summoned by the literary gods, Cynthia Shor appeared. She told us we'd have to come back tomorrow, but when she heard we lived 3,000 miles away and our flight home was leaving in the morning, she unlocked the door, and ushered us inside. "Let me grab an umbrella," she said, "and I'll give you a personal tour." She spent the next two hours, walking us from room to room, sharing history and local gossip.

I've taken lately to making postcard poems as thank you notes. They're easy to make, and serve as another way to spread poetry from the heart.

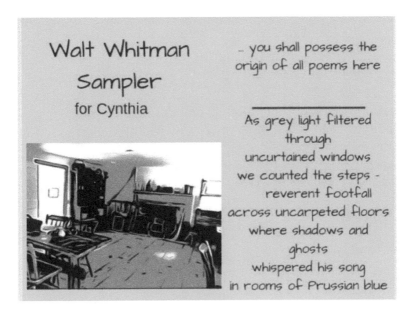

Walt Whitman
Sampler
for Cynthia

... you shall possess the
origin of all poems here

As grey light filtered
through
uncurtained windows
we counted the steps -
reverent footfall
across uncarpeted floors
where shadows and
ghosts
whispered his song
in rooms of Prussian blue

Invitation: Take a photo. Jot a few lines. Personalize it. Put a postcard stamp on the back along with the address. Voila. A postcard poem is on its way to make someone's day.

Prayer

Inspiration: The Irish writer, Samuel Beckett, is reported to have said "All poetry is prayer." After my father passed away in 2015, I began writing poems inspired by our relationship, which resulted in the publication of my poetry chapbook, *Avians of Mourning*. For me, my poems are prayers that honor the memories stitched together by the years of love.

Benediction

I learned to love the life-giving energy of earth from him
sun-burned Sundays spent on our knees
in the garden
digging bare-handed
gentling the roots
into safe spaces
patting dirt into tender brown mounds
sprinkling water as benediction

wiping rivulets of sweat from brows
broken nails on soil-crusted hands
we breathe in the moment
silent, reverent as we listen to a choir of songbirds
and the distant preaching of a crow

Song of Hope and Praise

rustle of sheets and the tiptoe
down the stairs at dawn

small glow from the bird lamp
bathing the hallway

slow drip of Italian coffee
into the waiting pot

eager pour of caffeinated elixir
swirled with almond milk

worn spot on the love seat
ritual begun in silent prayer

    doom scroll through the day's news

long centering walk
through the neighborhood

zoom calls and pretend hugs
mother, sister, daughters, babies

bare hands in the soft earth
and the ripening tomatoes

poems in the garden
books on the nightstand
words on my tongue

    We are better than this.
    We are more than this.
    Love will prevail.

    I still believe.

Invitation: Daily rituals can be prayerful. Consider those times when you work in silence alone or with a trusted other. Notice what it is that can be transcribed as a prayer, a time of spiritual communion and gratitude. Let that become your poem of thanks.

Protest

Inspiration: In November, 2016 I was attending a class at Harvard when the news broke. I wandered among my fellow citizens that day in stunned disbelief and sorrow. A few days later, I began to write, sitting outside a graveyard near campus. That next day, filling a notebook with thoughts, feelings, observations, reactions, hopes, I felt empowered. Awakened and ready to fight.

Of thee I sing

The sky is threatening rain today
this day after the day after the day after
still I travel on
aimlessly passing strangers
hugging signs and sorrows
heads down
eyes hooded,
lost in our collective quiet shame

In fading afternoon light
I pass a cemetery of the revolution
where thin and fragile tombstones
draped in dropped November leaves
stand as witness to our history,
America the Beautiful lies buried here
lost and restless deep below

Invitation: Your political views may be different than mine. No matter. There are things in the world that need to change. Write a poem of protest. Doesn't that feel good?

Quilt

Inspiration: I love old quilts. Like us, they are made of stories. I tried to sew a quilt once. Ended up with a bag of fabric strips and scraps stuffed on the top shelf of my closet where it lingered for years until I finally put it in a goodwill bag, hoping that someone could finish what I'd started. A quilt is not a quilt until it's stitched together. Lovingly.

A patchwork quilt poem is much easier to make, stitched together with words. These were made by pulling random lines from the poems gathered here in this collection, and rearranging to make something new.

Dawn

heavenly light
dances across this winter sky—
      gracefully hypnotic skydance

starlight swallows
shimmering air
sliver of fading moon

invisible forces
dropped from the skygod
into the night sky

first breath of morning
life bursting into light
streamed through stained glass

Late summer snapshot

ripening tomatoes
splattered with raindrops
sudden puddles
at the base of a giant redwood
fallen leaves, twisted trunks
fading afternoon light

Journey's End

thinkers and dreamers
sing a young man's song
hearts pounding wildly
longing for home
where rivers flow
with passionate intensity
and truth hides
in the shadows of the past

Invitation: Go to your bookshelves or the public library and gather up as many poetry books as your arms can hold. Grab another few for good measure. Spend an afternoon leafing through the books, searching for words and phrases that capture your heart. Jot them down until you fill a page or two. Mix and match until the words shape-shift into a poem of your own.

Rain

Inspiration: Rain is a mood-maker. It never fails in its ability to make you feel. Safe. Cold. Wet. Warm. Lonely. Loved. Rain becomes the background music to the moment. Whenever I hear rain on the roof, I'm ready to write.

Storm Warning

The birds understand
how today
the sky is a thick grey blanket
rippling in slow waves
releasing the unmistakable smell of *about to rain*

they were here this morning
among the roses
regaling with their sunshine songs until
they must have been cautioned by the wind
to pack up their belongings
and take a little daytrip

Me? I'm not so wind-tuned.
There I sat as the sky changed, lost, deep in the pages of my book
splattered with raindrops
listening for birds that were no longer there.

Into the Rain

Safeway parking lot
early morning, almost light
lone duck waddle-wanders
between the lines
across the vast,
through sudden puddles—
aimless and unhurried
while we rush past

Invitation: The next time you're awakened in the night by the tap tap of rain on the roof, or caught in a downpour without an umbrella, offer up a little prayer of thanks to the rainmaker, grab a pen and your notebook, and flood the page with a poetic response.

Rocks

Inspiration: When I was a child, we spent a week each summer at Lake Erie. At the end of a very long rocky beach, stood a huge rock sporting a painted mermaid, "The Lady on the Rock." I loved walking there with my father, talking about the bounty of nature and the beauty of the world. At home, he built a rock garden in our yard, while I planted geraniums and we chatted about birds. Rocks remind me of those times with him. I have a shelf filled with rocks, many heart-shaped, that I've gathered from places I've been. I love the heft and permanence of rocks and the way they remind me of walks and talks with my dad.

RIP

Early summer morning
I pause in my walk to pray
over this dead owl
face down in the dirt
soft feathers spread
like a summer blanket

Day after day
bird of wisdom and omen
remains silent untouched
no scavenger tears at the flesh
no curious cat bats it away

Road crew stops, mows around it

I pick up a flat rock
carry it home
take out my paints
soft grays and greens
a bit of mustardy yellow
for beak and eyes
winged life memorialized
on this miniature tombstone

for weeks they remain there together

flesh and feather, bone and stone

Invitation: Painted rocks, magic rocks, kindness rocks, and rocks bearing signs and symbols are everywhere these days, left as anonymous messages of hope and connection. Paint a message on a rock as a poem. Leave it for someone to find. And if you'd like, you can write a poem about it too. Double the joy!

Setting

Inspiration: Sometimes a place becomes a poem. When I walked into Teddy Roosevelt's estate on the North Shore of Long Island, it felt like I had stepped back in time. Here at his summer White House, surrounded by reminders of his oversized personality, curiosity, and intellect, I made note of what was on display, and the poem just wrote itself.

Thoughts While Visiting Teddy's House at Sagamore

From the wrap-around porch we step into the foyer,
paying no heed to
elephant tusks,
Samurai swords,
and heads of beasts on display
we turn our attention
to his book-lined study, where it's said he read a volume a day
   This book-lined study from which he led the country,
calling statesmen and learned men to his side
for debate and counsel
where Greek and Latin rolled off the tongue; German and French were
second nature, and the English language was revered.
Notice how book-lined shelves fill nearly every room here, hallmarks of a
curious mind.
Evenings, he recited poetry at the family table,
his children conversing with the thinkers and dreamers of the day—
Edison and Ford inspired invention and possibility,
hope and wonder.
Now, contrast that with the current resident of the highest office in the land,
who cannot even master his own tongue, who reads nothing of substance
or depth,
who gorges on cable tv, who hangs with liars and thieves,
thick with cowardice and greed.
And you ask me why I grieve?

Invitation:
When you visit someplace, be it a historical landmark or the corner grocery store, carry a notebook, and look with new eyes. Jot down your noticings, your feelings, overheard conversations, unexpected connections. Turn your jottings into a poem that is as clear and remarkable as a photograph.

Small Poems

Inspiration: Kevin Hodgson is a poet I've only met through Twitter. In October, 2019, he posted a twitter invitation to participate in a collaborative small poem project. The instructions were simple: "Grab a slide, write a small poem, share a picture." That was it. I shared a photograph from my father's gravesite that I'd visited that morning, along with a quickly composed haiku.

Among the fallen leaves
Where his scattered ashes fell
Stone angel brings peace

Invitation: It's simple. Scroll through the photos on your phone, and find one that catches your eye, sparks a powerful memory, or causes your heart to flip-flop. Use that photo as inspiration to craft a small poem, the smaller the better. You might want to try several small poems sparked by that one photo, or select several photos for a series of small poems.

Time

Inspiration: The City of San Ramon built a new city hall a few years ago. I wrote a poem about the initial ground breaking. A year later I wrote a dedication poem for the new building. A year after that, the city council buried a time capsule in the cement at the building's entrance, to be opened in 2083, long after I'm gone. Inside that capsule is a book of poems I wrote during my tenure as Poet Laureate. Poems about history, and neighbors, and local events—a chronicle of our time here. I love knowing that my grandchildren may come here with their grandchildren in 2083, to see the time capsule opened, to hear my voice welcoming them to a time before.

The sweet swift passage of time

outside my window yesterday
old tree stood, tall and proud
waving its branches
winter bare
as the rains came down
and the winds came up
shivering the day

today the sun of nearly spring
awakened me
and this old tree
standing silently still outside
casting long shadows,
limbs lifted skyward as if in prayer
budded now all white and leafy green

in the world beyond the trees
it's hard to practice the fine art
of noticing,
remembering that between yesterday
and tomorrow
there is just this now, this unclaimed moment
where teacher trees reveal
what wasn't there before

I'm learning now
to slowly see
the sweet swift passage of time
to love
how the seasons shift
in the narrow spaces
between dark and dawn

Reverie

September air, subtle season shifts
reddening, readying leaves for change
graceful bird shadows
waltz high above my perch
red-headed woodpecker
taps out his autumn song
time   time   time   time
transporting me back
to Papa's garden
beneath tall pines
slow bee buzz
and my first woodpecker concert
Papa in his suspendered jeans,
jamming with the chorus
tapping out time on a rusty trash can

Time travel

Strapped into a metal cylinder
Hurtling across the sky
Through blue and cloud and nothingness
Thoughts drift future forward
Till with a jolt we land

Thrust into this space
Where everything new
Is familiar still
Shadows of the past
Grow distant

Memories of other days
Blur into
This here and now
Until once again we fly

Invitation: Time is that mysterious thread that connects past and future. Sometimes it feels like looking through a blurred kaleidoscope of interchangeable moments. Moments upon moments, some linked in the stories we tell ourselves, some locked away until a sound or a smell awakens our senses and shakes free a memory. When a memory surfaces, grab your notebook, and make it into a poem.

Unexpected

Inspiration: For years I've chronicled people I run into unexpectedly in a special journal just for that purpose. I log the date, the place, the circumstances of our unexpected reunion. I'm looking for patterns. Was I thinking about them recently? Did they appear in a dream or in a conversation with a friend? Was the universe trying to send me a message?

Chance Meeting

Turn the corner, there you are
in the canned goods aisle at Safeway
or a crowded restroom at O'Hare
small roadside diner in Jersey
sidewalk café in Paris

a startle
　　　　and then
　　　　　　　　the melt of
long years

in my journal
I note date and time
each simple circumstance
each detail recounted
life story captured
in bold bullet points

what invisible forces
pull us toward such
unplanned encounters
universe of possibilities

　　　　step inside
　　　　this time machine

　　　　　　turn the corner
　　　　　　　again
　　　　　　　　　go our separate ways

Invitation: When you have a chance meeting with someone, don't let it go unnoticed. Chances are you've thought about that person recently. Maybe even dreamed about them, or checked them out on social media. Jot down the circumstances of your encounter; turn it into a poem.

Virus

Inspiration: It's impossible to escape the impact of the 2020 global pandemic. Ubiquitous, seeping into every waking moment of our lives. All our hopes and dreams. I think about it constantly, duel emotions of hope and fear. Action plan: I can wear a mask. I can keep a safe distance. I can write a poem.

Nature Doesn't Seem to Know or Care

The azaleas are in riotous bloom
a profusion of pinks and reds
their wind-driven petals scattered
across the walkway
to our front door
a floral carpet no one will cross

Out back the roses are showing off
their first shy buds opening
yellow and peach and red
oblivious to the fact
that there will be
no garden party here this spring

Meanwhile, two neighborhood cats
are perched upon the fence
facing each other
tails swishing slowly
shaking loose the wisteria blossoms
onto the playground behind our house
the stage is set for a catfight
that the schoolchildren will not hear

Between the press conferences
and the daily news
silently we wait
while the rain falls
and the flowers bloom

Privilege

Late afternoon on the 40th day
my husband donned
cotton mask and gardening gloves
his new uniform
for the short drive to the market

one large cardboard box,
a miracle bounty
farm-fresh-filled
loaded into our trunk
by a stranger in protective gear

on our kitchen counter
I carefully removed
potatoes, tomatoes, jalapeños, carrots, squash,
red onions, blueberries, strawberries, avocados,
lemons, limes, bunches of leafy green lettuce

washed each offering
roots and leaves and skins
patted dry
gentled all into bowls and bins
murmuring a song of gratitude
for those who made it so

today, waking to a symphony of birds
praise song for this day ahead
baking bread
reading in the garden
writing longhand letters
aware, at last, of what it means to be lucky
what it means to be

The Upside

The pandemic has confined me to the garden
This garden, after years of neglect

is a profusion of lovely today
flowering hydrangea spill out of their pots
delighting swooping swallowtail
and songbirds drunk on floral wine
Here, towering tomato vines reach
for twisted wisteria buzzing with bees
and two lemon trees bearing first fruit
Here, an explosion of roses snakes up the trellis
I sit beneath. Here too, my notebook,
keeper of ideas that bloom and fade,
is bursting with new life, a fruitful bible
spilling stories across pages
grown newly alive with promise

Invitation: Whether it's a virus or some other catastrophic happening, we can always make sure to respond in ways that lift others up. Take whatever positive action you can, of course—and that includes sharing poetry. A poem always helps.

Walking

Inspiration: As a writer, I find I spend a lot of time sitting. It's easy to get lost in the work and forget to come up for air, so I set a little timer and make myself take little walks. I vary my route and always take my phone along for capturing interesting sites—a little photo journaling, if you will. I'm looking for metaphors in the making.

Autumn Walk at Daybreak

setting out
before first light
wrapped in cold
and still silent dark

spirit awakened
earth-tuned
beneath heavy pines
and this sliver of fading moon
shadowing a great horned owl

spirit awakened
sudden flap of wings
from above
and beyond
signaling change, perhaps

rounding the corner
they are already here

the workmen
come from far away
under cover of darkness
to lie in wait
in their rusty Hondas
while the neighbors rise
creatures of habit
get in their fancy cars
heading somewhere else

believing
they are obeying
the natural order of things

Idolatry

Walking through the neighborhood
of the blessed, sentinel statues
grace green expanses leading home
Mother Mary, hands folded in prayer
Three carved angels playing
flute, harp, lute, their music
trapped in stone
on the doorstep, right hand raised
Buddha sits, protecting all who enter
and Lord Krishna rests among the hedges
St. Francis waits at the garden gate
bedecked with birds of welcome
and up the road a bit, a winged
Archangel stands towering
over the rhododendrons
richly trumpeting
You've made it home

Invitation: Walking is the best way I know to pay attention to the world. Lace up your sneakers. Go as far as you can go, filing images away on your phone or in the camera of your mind. When you return, first stretch, then get busy writing. Let the poems flow, released like endorphins.

X Marks the Spot

Inspiration: In the summer of 2020, in the midst of the pandemic that had us confined to home, I was granted the opportunity to write at Eugene O'Neill's tranquil estate called Tao House. This is the spot, high in the hills of my hometown, where the Pulitzer Prize-winning playwright composed his most famous works. I had the place to myself for days. At Tao House, I was completely alone, except I really was not—I felt his presence everywhere.

Solitude

There is an old trunk room
on the playwright's estate
where I'm typing these lines
just for you

I've wandered the grounds
ambled through the old barn
read my fill in the library, quietly
crammed ceiling to floor
with dusty old tomes
dying to speak

I've prayed at a tombstone
beneath an old walnut tree
marking the spot on a hill
where he buried his heart
along with his dog
a very long time ago

I've watched a lone hawk
circling slow overhead
a gracefully hypnotic skydance
while lizards sunbathe
and rattlesnakes laze
and the touch of the poet remains

O'Neill

This is the house where he wrote the words,
Yes, there's the making of a poet in you, all right
and here I sit in the window where he once sat
serenaded by treetop wrens,
ancestors of birds that warbled and chirped
as he conjured Mary and Tyrone in passion's heat.
Here I sit, beneath the twisted trunks of elm and oak
where he once sat
drinking in the breeze
thinking, *The past is the present, isn't it?*
It's the future too.
Here, slow brown cows are lowing
beyond beloved Blemie's grave
And here I sit in shadow, nodding to the past
pastoral peace above the freeway's roar
a poet's long day's musings.

Invitation: Find a quiet place where you can be alone with your thoughts. Spend as big a chunk of time as possible there, going back as often as you can. Feel the spirit of the place in your bones. Write.

Yeats

Inspiration: Years ago, in my undergraduate days, I took a course from Professor William Dumbleton that changed my life. His course was part research, part storytelling, part recitation, and all heart. I fell in love with Yeats, who remains my favorite to this day, when Professor Dumbleton recited *The Second Coming*. Decades later, I cannot read the poem without rerunning the scene that played out in the classroom that day.

The Second Coming (Revisiting Yeats)

It was the '70s
Professor Dumbleton stood
at the front of the classroom
reciting a poem from memory

His back to us
chalk dust flying
with passionate intensity
as he spiraled *the widening gyre*
across the board

Things fall apart;
the centre cannot hold

And here we are again

In the midst of a pandemic
One man stands at the podium, unmasked

In the midst of peaceful protests
One man brandishes a bible, unrepentant

In the midst of endless suffering
One man sends a tweet, unhinged

Things fall apart;
the centre cannot hold

Things fall apart;
the centre cannot hold

The time has come
Our time has come

We are coming together to hold
each other
together

Invitation: Surely, you've had the experience of hearing a poem read, or a song sung for the first time that has made an indelible mark on you. Whenever you come across it again, you flash back to that first experience. Capture one of those moments, and write a poem connecting it to here and now.

Zoom

Inspiration: In the age of Zoom, I've moved my writing classes on-line. In one session with fifth grade girls, they were writing fast and furious, heads down, fingers flying, capturing ideas before the timer went off. Writing in silence, locked behind screens, feeling the power of shared passions in this virtual space.

We had just engaged in a conversation about our writing identities. Brooke said, "I'm a writer who writes with deep emotion, trying to figure out the world and my place in it." Whoa! "I'm the kind of writer who likes to create big conflicts and then work all the angles to solve them," said Blair. And Alexa astutely said, "I'm the kind of writer who always has ideas and starts stories with a lot of excitement, but I lose momentum easily after a page or two."

Spoiler Alert

The spell is broken.
One of the girls, the one trying to figure out her place in the world, spots a spider on her keyboard. A small one. Jumping from key to key. We're all on mute, but we feel her jump up. We hear her silent scream.
Unmuted now.
"Don't kill it!" says the one who likes to solve problems. "Shoo it off your keyboard and cover it with a cup. Make sure it's clear so you can keep your eye on it."
"Go get your sister," says the one with lots of ideas.
"Why don't you work on your descriptions using metaphor?" says you know who.
A spider is a web-weaver. A spell-breaker. A mood-shifter. A story-starter. A story-ender.

Invitation: Bring your imagination to your next on-line meeting. Consider the focus of the gathering. Don't focus on that. Pay attention to the other things going on instead. Recount the details in a poem.

That's it, my poet friends.

Artifacts, birds, ghosts, rocks, and rain.

Everyday poetry sparks.

Life's recurring refrains.

I hope you found some inspiration in the invitations here
across these pages.

I wish you and poetry a long and happy life together.

#POETRYLOVE

Kate McCarroll Moore is a collector of stories, discarded objects, and memories. She is a mentor teacher, book coach, and staff developer who served three terms as Poet Laureate for the City of San Ramon. Kate holds a Doctorate in Educational Leadership for Social Justice and she uses her passion for poetry to promote kindness, empathy, and connection. She was an education columnist for several years and has had her poetry published in numerous journals and anthologies. Currently serving as a book coach for a non-profit organization that connects low-income families with access to high quality books, Kate teaches online writing classes and has studied with Naomi Shihab Nye, Tess Taylor, Georgia Heard among other poets. She is the author of the chapbook, *Avians of Mourning*, as well as two middle grade novels. Kate is grateful for her East Coast roots, and loves living with her husband in northern California where the sky is always blue, the birds are always singing, the garden is always beckoning, and her children and grandchildren are always close by.

CPSIA information can be obtained
at www.ICGtesting.com
Printed in the USA
LVHW072251180322
713836LV00007B/37

9 781646 627929